Jake

the Jail Bird

"A voice is a song if you use it.
A fall is a flight if you choose it."

Balboa Press books may be ordered through booksellers or by contacting:

Balboa Press
A Division of Hay House
1663 Liberty Drive
Bloomington, IN 47403
www.balboapress.com
844-682-1282

ISBN: 978-1-9822-7292-0 (sc)
ISBN: 978-1-9822-7293-7 (e)

Library of Congress Control Number: 2021916209

Print information available on the last page.

Balboa Press rev. date: 08/09/2021

BALBOA.PRESS
A DIVISION OF HAY HOUSE

Jake
the Jail Bird

Emily Bowles

Illustrated by Devin Painter

If you look up very closely, you will see that there's a highway in the sky. You won't see lanes or trains, but you will see pilots and planes. You'll find cumulus clouds and precipitation, occasionally running into a construction zone full of thunder and lightning. Amidst all of the traffic, however, you might spot a feathered friend. To and fro, here and there, feathers and air. Even when it seems that you are alone, if you look up and all you see is blue, just close your eyes and listen. You'll hear a joyful tune. Some say that wings carry messages from the heavens, and if this is true, our birds have an important job to do, as do me and you.

This is the story of Jake. He was just a baby when he earned his name. A little too early, some would say. But when it comes to destiny there is only one way.

Jake's life began as any other bird's, from inside of an egg. And in this hollow place, from pure silence, music was made. With one crack in the shell, Jake's song met the air that momentous day. He opened his eyes to greet his mother and father's gaze. At first, Jake longed for his mother's heartbeat, frantically fearing the heavy weight. But just as he opened his beak to object, his mother embraced him with her warmth and Jake settled into his new nest.

As days would pass, Jake grew and grew. The love of Mom and Dad, Jake always knew. The magic of flight carrying him food, and he always found it fascinating how the other birds flew. Though it was certain that his time to fly would come, every morning Jake awoke to a brilliant sun. With each shining rise the skies yearned for his song, until Jake finally met the moment that awaited him for so long.

Now strong and fit, (as a fiddle, some would say), Jake felt an air of nervous excitement to the skies that day. This entire flock of songbirds, a family of Jays, celebrated with daring stunts and singing tunes of praise. Safety checks, the flight was set. Calculations had been made. The clouds were calling Jake. Yet in his fragile young bird bones, even with his family cheering him on, he still felt mighty alone.

The pressure was building. The world seemed so vast. Was he ready to parachute into this new role being cast? "Everyone's watching," he thought with recall. "They fly with grace. But I might be too small. And what if I fall?"

So he made a vow to do his best, closed his eyes and took a breath. And with just one single step, Jake left the nest. With the wind carrying him, at first glance he flew fine. Until suddenly the spectacle drastically declined. Jake took a dive.

From their various branches and perches, the other birds grew alarmed. So they sprang into action with synchronized song. Their efforts were tough, coordinated, and slick. Though Jake was slender and he free-fell quick. During the fall, Jake was in shock. He closed his eyes and his beak and let go without any thought.

The powerful wind took him astray, as his distraught flock hopelessly watched Jake's landing spot with dismay. There were tall buildings and trees, and lots of empty space. Yet Jake fell through the cracks into a chain-link cage.

The sign read "Corrections", though the birds didn't care. They were creatures of flight, freedom and air. Their hearts ached for young Jake, still on the ground. He lay all alone, with four tall walls all around. What will they do now?

When Jake finally awoke, it was to a loud clash, with no way of knowing how much time had passed. He opened his eyes and the world was one he had never before seen. The only thing familiar being the sunshine in between. He didn't know where he was. He had no idea how to get home. Yet his heart spoke to his head and said, "It's not over. Keep on. Go."

But now there was movement, a peculiar sound. And then came vibrations all around with footsteps on the ground. And he met the eyes of a curious figure looking down. The being was limber, round, and tall. She began to crawl on hands and knees to humbly kneel at the scene of his fall.

"Hey little bird, Are you hurt?" The girl whispered. Jake didn't speak English, but he could sense her concern. He noticed her begin to examine his bruises. She assessed that despite the mess, Jake wasn't broken. He immediately felt safe with the girl, because her heart was open. Then suddenly, Jake heard a flurry of human commotion.

That's when a crowd began to gather. All concerned for the baby bird, they rushed to see what was the matter. Jake didn't notice their jumpsuits, because all he saw was light, emanating from their hearts. They shined so very bright. And they brought him water to drink from a small plastic cap. Although he had no use for words, their compassion bridged the gap.

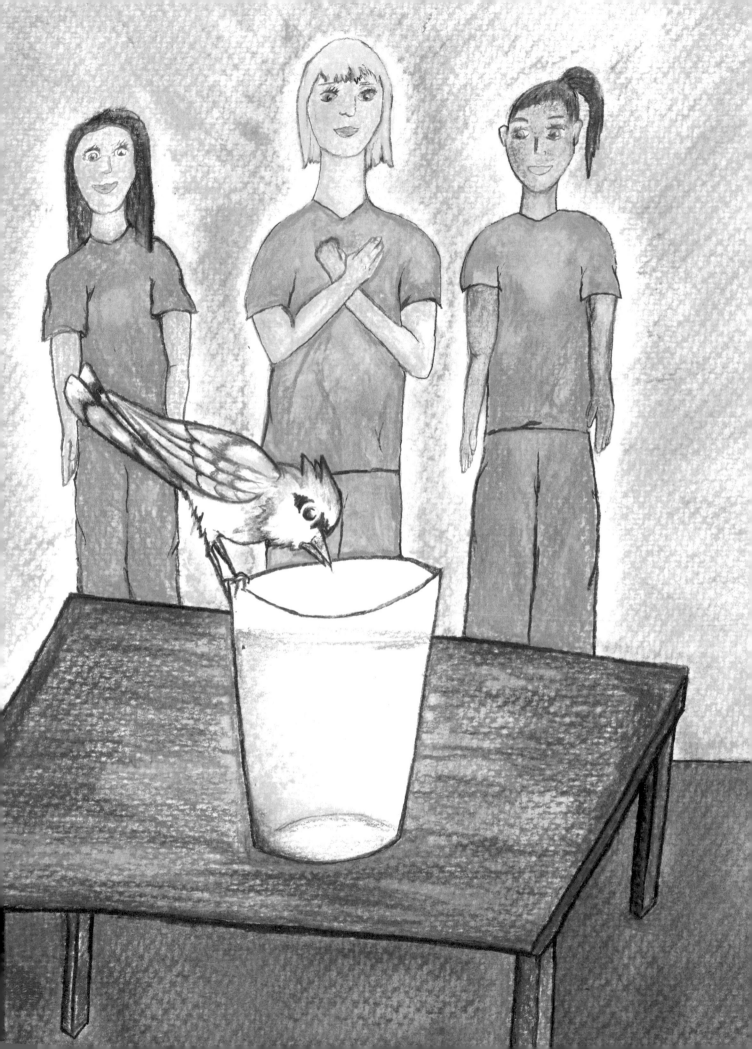

A familiar sound pricked Jake's ears. It immediately quieted most of his fears. A brilliant song was being sung from up high. As these women prisoners lifted their heads to the sky, they saw Jake's loyal tribe.

At the sight of Jake's fall, his mother and father had taken an immediate descent, to perch on the roof of a chain link fence. They found a square box, with holes for air to move through,

but all were too small to fit Mom and Pop Jay Blue. So now all that they could possibly do is deliver love, encouragement, and food, from a distance, watching over young Jake. Until he was strong enough to make his jail break.

As the day's passed, Jake began to understand that everyone in this place was part of a grander plan. And if it were a space of punishment, well he was there too. Completely blameless, just looking for a way through. It did not make sense, how these women fit, in cages so small, with bright bodies so big. According to him, they were all innocent. And he became more than a pet to them. He was a guide, a teacher, a friend. They tenderly cared for Jake, as day turned to night and night into day. He patiently rested and had dreams of flying away.

But then Jake grew restless about a feeling in the air. He couldn't quite explain it, but still he sensed something there. A calling, a pressure, an urgent melody. He waited for a sure sign that it was time to leave. Watching the ladies week after week, he begged and pleaded for reprieve with every single peep.

Finally, it seemed there would be no relief, by the hands of these people or in the singing wind and trees. The universe was waiting on Jake to make his move. Which route would he take, and when would he choose?

So he began training by taking small flights. He would make it halfway, and then descend for the night. Each day he practiced lifting up, and then down. His efforts were met with applause all around. He began to see how his jail time could be a part of a grand design. He knew that his purpose was alive deep within, and all he could do now was fulfill his mission.

Eventually, Jake started feeling stronger. He learned that falling was easy, but getting up takes longer. And although he had tried and failed in the past, it was time to courageously take another chance.

The day had come for Jake's redemption. He knew there were no guarantees. He would take this flight on his own. His body had grown, he was no longer a baby. With courage in his heart, he stepped up to play his part.

The sun was not shining. The skies were pure gray. The clouds looked ominous, but that was not enough to sway Jake. His adopted family of women watched in awe, and from above they heard a loud squaw. Jake's parents were there, excited as ever. And it became true that birds of a feather flock together, no matter the weather.

Once again Jake heard those words in his mind. "But what if you fall?" And with bravery, Jake exclaimed, "But what if I fly?"

And just like that, Jake took off strong. He scaled the wall, went through the fence, and then soared on. The other birds joined him with glorious praise. And the skies rained joy that one epic day when Jake, from prison, flew away.

Printed in the United States
by Baker & Taylor Publisher Services